THIS BOOK BELONGS TO

- -

HOW TO USE THIS BOOK

1

Find the **sticker page** which matches the scene.

2

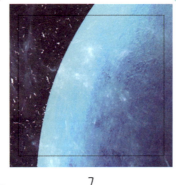

7

Pay attention to the **number** under each sticker!

3

Match the stickers to the numbers on the **grid** to complete the picture.

7

WHAT CAN WE FIND IN SPACE?

Space is the huge, dark, mostly empty place between all the different objects existing in our universe. Here are a few things we could find in space!

STARS

Stars are made of really hot gas, and they shine brightly in space. Our sun is a star.

PLANETS

Planets are big balls of matter that go around stars. We live on a planet: Earth!

Comets are made of ice and rock. They turn to gas as they get closer to the sun, and leave behind a streaky trail.

COMETS

What we call 'shooting stars' are actually meteors! When stuff from space enters Earth's atmosphere, it burns up, shooting through the sky.

MOONS

Moons are objects that move around planets. We only have one moon orbiting Earth, but some planets have dozens!

METEORS

THE SUN

THE SUN is the <u>star</u> at the <u>center</u> of our solar system. **Everything** in the solar system <u>revolves</u> around it, so its pretty important!

THE SUN IS MORE THAN 4 BILLION YEARS OLD!

solar flares which are like <u>explosions</u> of light

the sun is a <u>giant ball</u> made of **plasma**

the **core** of the sun is the <u>hottest</u> part

the sun is the **largest object** in our <u>solar system</u>

1	2	3	4	5
6	7	8	9	10
11	12	13	14	15
16	17	18	19	20

 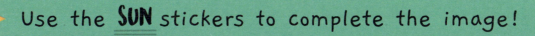 Use the **SUN** stickers to complete the image!

EARTH

EARTH is the **planet** we call our **home.** It rotates every **twenty-four hours**, giving us about twelve hours of **daylight** and twelve hours of **night!**

EARTH HAS A POPULATION OF OVER 8 BILLION PEOPLE!

70% of Earth's surface is made of water

large pieces of land are called **continents**

oceans make over half of the oxygen we breathe!

Earth spins around the sun

1	2	3	4	5
6	7	8	9	10
11	12	13	14	15
16	17	18	19	20

 Use the **EARTH** stickers to complete the image!

MERCURY

MERCURY is the **closest** planet to the sun and the **smallest** planet in our **solar system.** It can be **spotted** from Earth before the sun rises and after the sun sets.

A YEAR ON MERCURY IS ONLY 88 EARTH DAYS!

the **temperature** can get both ver**y** hot and ver**y** cold

short and **fast** **orbit** around the sun

rocky surface with deep **craters** and high **cliffs**

its only a **little** **bigger** than our moon

1	2	3	4	5
6	7	8	9	10
11	12	13	14	15
16	17	18	19	20

 Use the **MERCURY** stickers to complete the image!

ROCKET

ROCKETS burn **fuel** to launch **spacecraft** into space. They can travel **hundreds** of miles in a minute and their **engines** are extremely hot!

THE LARGEST ROCKET IS OVER 300 FEET TALL!

pointed nose to control **direction** in space

rocket fins for **stability** after **take-off**

special chamber which **burns fuel**

hot gases shoot out the **back** of the rocket

1	2	3	4	5
6	7	8	9	10
11	12	13	14	15
16	17	18	19	20

 Use the **ROCKET** stickers to complete the image!

URANUS

URANUS is the seventh planet from the sun and the **coldest** planet in our **solar system.** Some areas on its surface don't get **sunlight** for over **forty-two years.** That's quite a long time!

A DAY ON URANUS IS THE SAME AS 84 YEARS ON EARTH!

pale blue colour due to methane gas

13 faint rings surround Uranus

this planet is a ball of **swirling** ice and **gas**

Uranus is the only planet which rotates on its side

1	2	3	4	5
6	7	8	9	10
11	12	13	14	15
16	17	18	19	20

 Use the <u>URANUS</u> stickers to complete the image!

VENUS

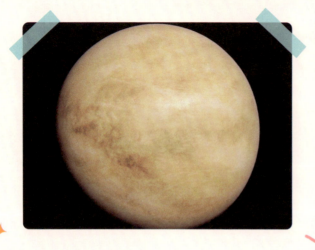

VENUS is the **closest** planet to Earth and the **hottest** planet in our **solar system**, with temperatures on the surface reaching as **high** as 480°C!

VENUS IS THE SECOND BRIGHTEST OBJECT IN OUR SKY!

spins in the **opposite direction** to Earth

yellow clouds made of **deadly acid**

solid surface that is covered in **volcanoes**

scorching temperature so it doesn't **rain**

1	2	3	4	5
6	7	8	9	10
11	12	13	14	15
16	17	18	19	20

Use the **VENUS** stickers to complete the image!

NEPTUNE

NEPTUNE is the **furthest** planet from the sun and can only be seen from **Earth** through a **telescope.** It is a very **cold** and very **dark** planet.

NEPTUNE IS 4 TIMES WIDER THAN EARTH!

Neptune has 14 different moons

freezing cold temperatures as it is far from the sun

there is **no surface:** the blue that we see is gas clouds

wind speeds are 9 times stronger than on Earth!

1	2	3	4	5
6	7	8	9	10
11	12	13	14	15
16	17	18	19	20

 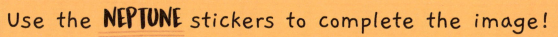

Use the **NEPTUNE** stickers to complete the image!

MARS

MARS is the **fourth** planet from the sun, also known as the **red planet** because of its **rusty colour**. It is also the **only** other planet we may eventually be able to **live** on!

DUST STORMS ON MARS CAN LAST FOR MONTHS!

gravity means you weigh less on Mars

the **surface** is very hard and rocky

the **average temparature** is about −62°C... Brrr!

the **biggest volcano** on Mars is 25km tall!

	2	3	4	5
6	7	8	9	10
11	12	13	14	15
16	17	18	19	20

 Use the **MARS** stickers to complete the image!

JUPITER

JUPITER is sometimes referred to as the '**King of the Planets**' as it is the **largest** planet in our **solar system**. It is **bigger** than all of the other planets **combined**!

A STORM HAS BEEN RAGING ON JUPITER FOR 350 YEARS!

Jupiter is made of only liquids and gases

Jupiter has 79 moons

its **extreme storms** can be seen from space

a **day** on Jupiter is only 10 hours long!

1	2	3	4	5
6	7	8	9	10
11	12	13	14	15
16	17	18	19	20

Use the **JUPITER** stickers to complete the image!

SATURN

SATURN is the **second largest** planet in our **solar system**. It is called the **jewel** of our solar system because of the beautiful **rings** which surround it.

SATURN IS THE LIGHTEST OF ALL THE PLANETS!

Saturn's **rings** are made of ice, dust and rock

there are 7 **main rings** around Saturn

Saturn has more **moons** than any other planet!

Saturn **travels** around the sun very slowly

1
2
3
4
5
6
7
8
9
10
11
12
13
14
15
16
17
18
19
20

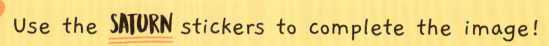

Use the **SATURN** stickers to complete the image!

SATELLITES

SATELLITES are man-made objects which are sent to orbit planets or stars. They gather information and transmit it back to Earth. How clever!

SATELLITES TRAVEL AT 18,000 MILES AN HOUR!

solar panels use energy from sunlight in space

the control centre receives instructions and signals

sensors for guidance and direction

antennas to communicate with Earth

1	2	3	4	5
6	7	8	9	10
11	12	13	14	15
16	17	18	19	20

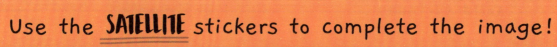

Use the **SATELLITE** stickers to complete the image!

SOLAR SYSTEM

OUR SOLAR SYSTEM is an incredible place that consists of <u>**eight planets**</u> centred around <u>**the sun**</u>. It is about <u>**four and a half billion years**</u> old! <u>**Earth**</u> is the only planet in the system known to contain <u>**life**</u>.

The sun is one of 200 billion stars

THERE ARE ALSO 6 DWARF PLANETS IN THE SOLAR SYSTEM!

The sun

Mercury

Earth

Venus

Mars

Jupiter

Saturn

Uranus

Neptune

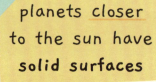

planets <u>closer</u> to the sun have **solid surfaces**

planets <u>further</u> from the sun are called **gas giants**

Neptune's location was predicted by <u>mathematicians</u>

1	2	3	4	5
6	7	8	9	10
11	12	13	14	15
16	17	18	19	20

Use the **SOLAR SYSTEM** stickers to complete the image!

Can you find the SOLAR SYSTEM words?

L	S	A	S	E	R	P
T	T	V	A	A	A	L
S	A	T	U	R	N	A
T	R	P	N	T	E	N
A	K	X	R	H	M	E
S	P	A	C	E	S	T
E	M	O	O	N	I	P

EARTH   SATURN   STAR

SPACE   MOON   PLANET

CIRCLE THE ODD PLANET OUT!

Match the SPACE words to their pictures!

METEOR   ROCKET   EARTH

Help the **ROCKET** find its way back to **EARTH**!

Spot 5 differences between the SPACE scenes!

SUN STICKERS

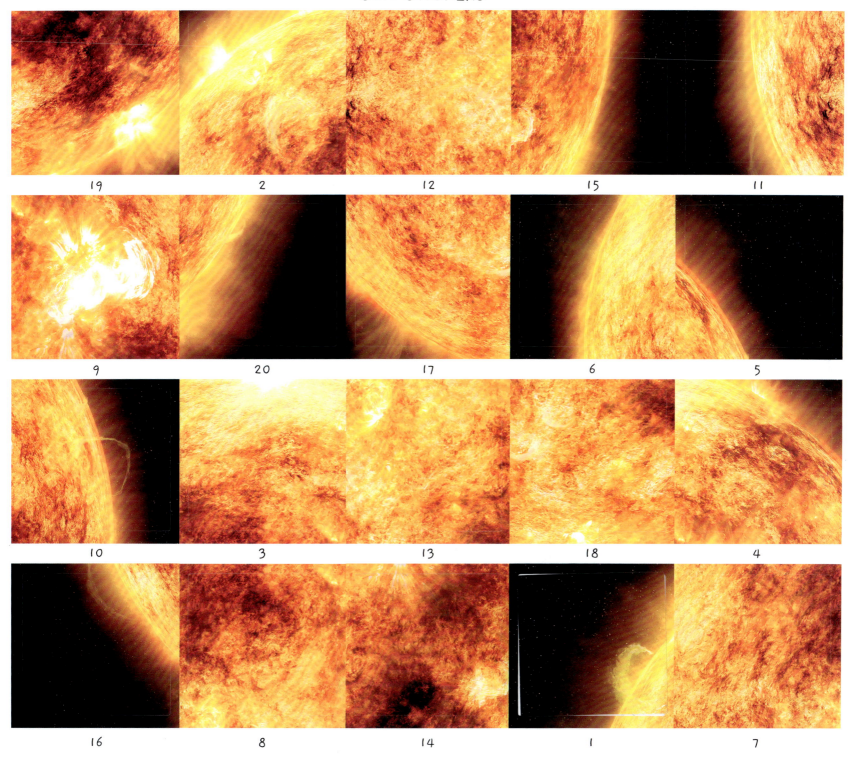

EARTH STICKERS

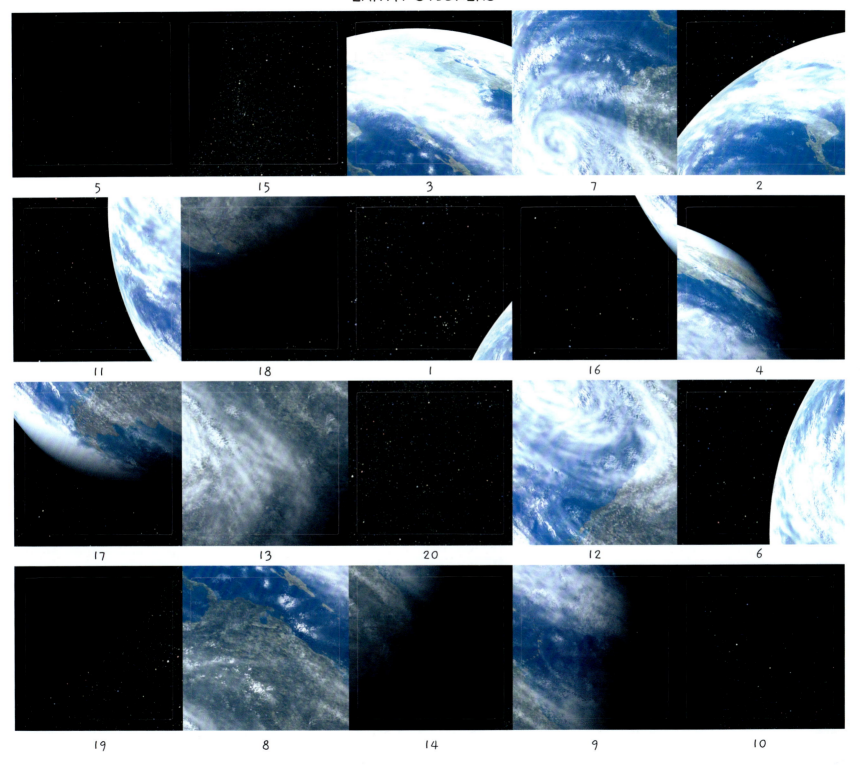

5

15

3

7

2

11

18

1

16

4

17

13

20

12

6

19

8

14

9

10

MERCURY STICKERS

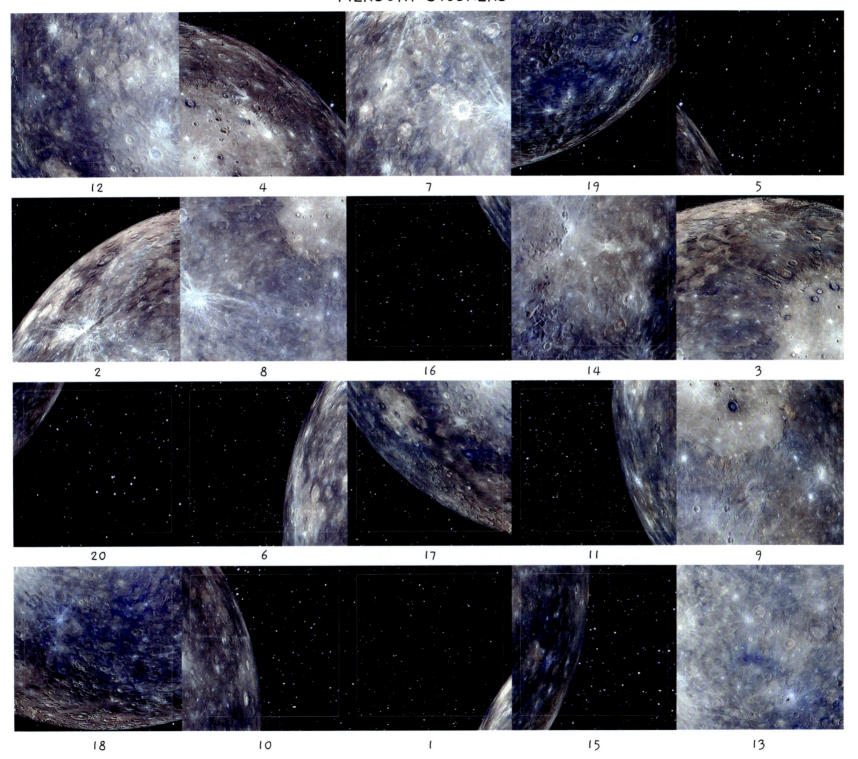

12   4   7   19   5

2   8   16   14   3

20   6   17   11   9

18   10   1   15   13

ROCKET STICKERS

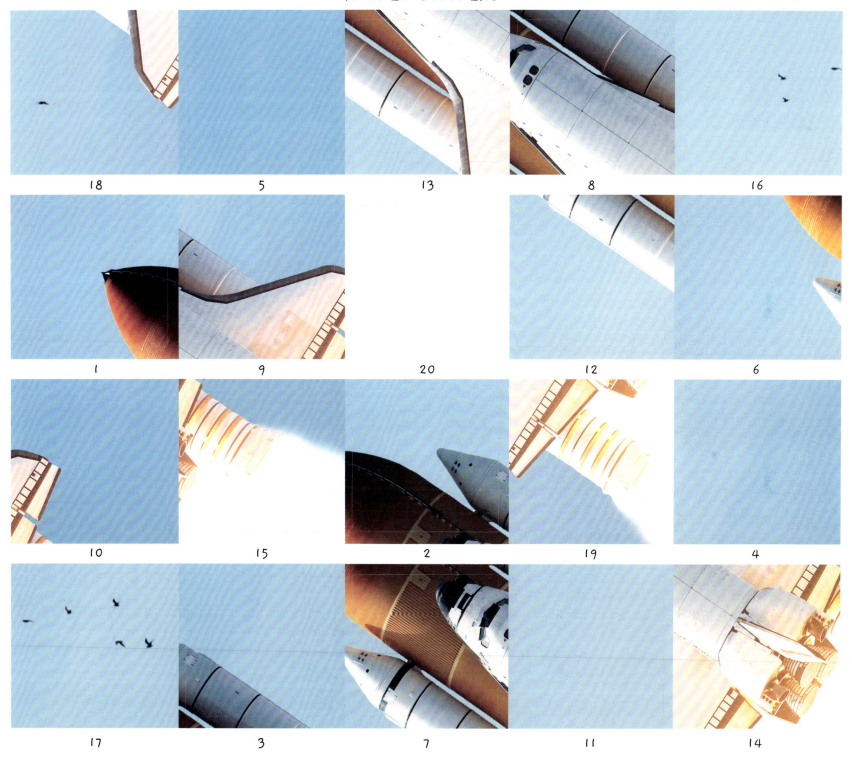

18 5 13 8 16

1 9 20 12 6

10 15 2 19 4

17 3 7 11 14

URANUS STICKERS

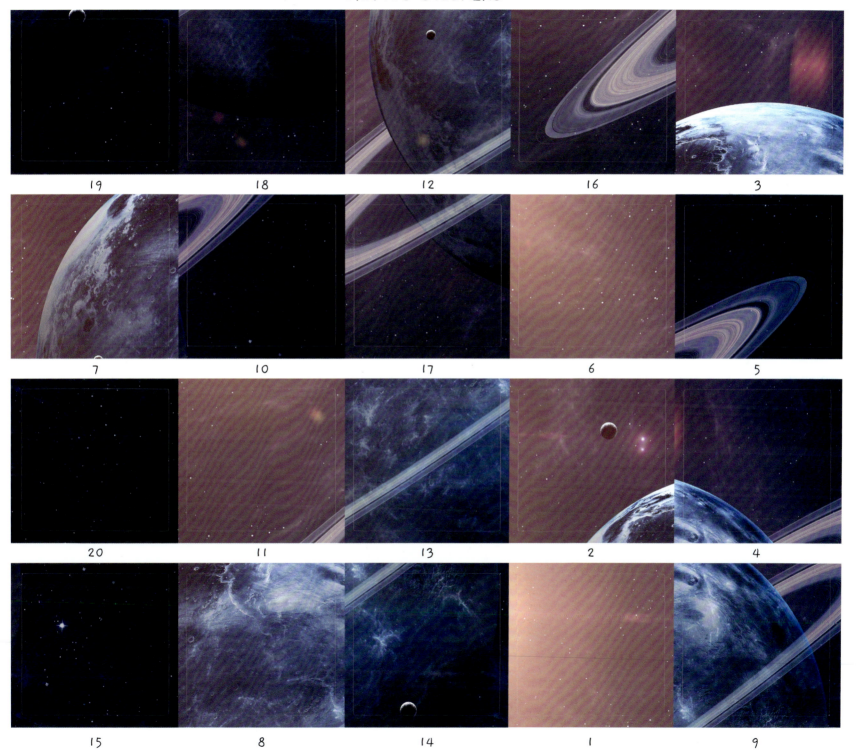

VENUS STICKERS

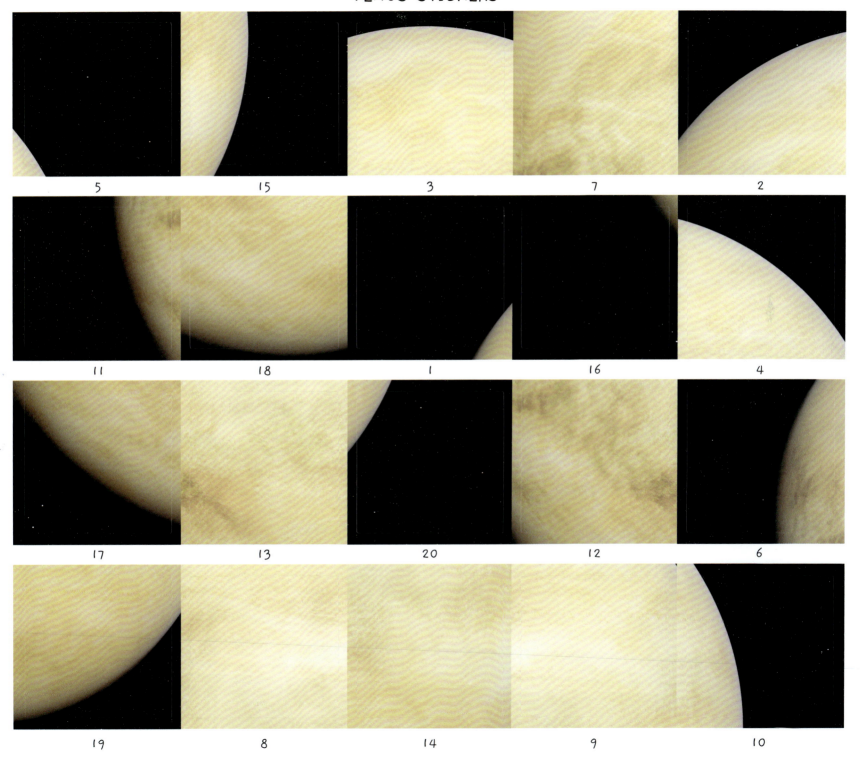

NEPTUNE STICKERS

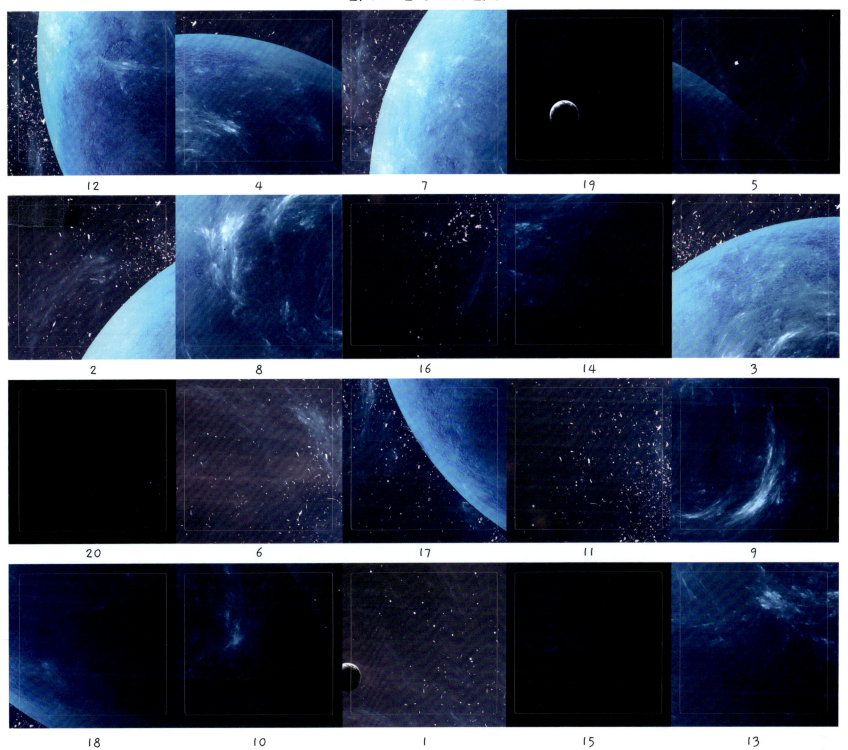

12   4   7   19   5

2   8   16   14   3

20   6   17   11   9

18   10   1   15   13

MARS STICKERS

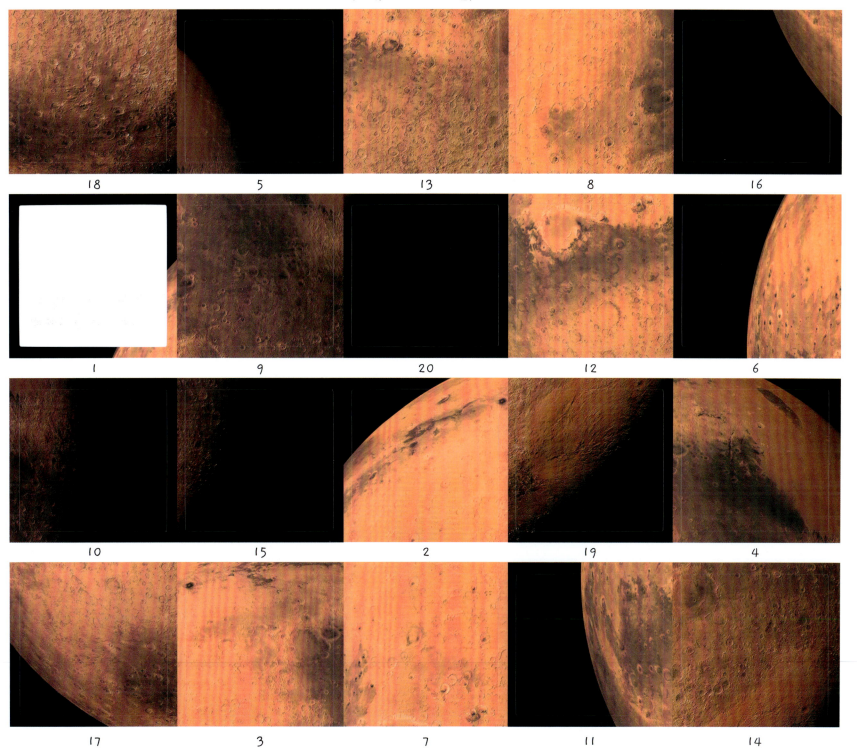

18

5

13

8

16

1

9

20

12

6

10

15

2

19

4

17

3

7

11

14

JUPITER STICKERS

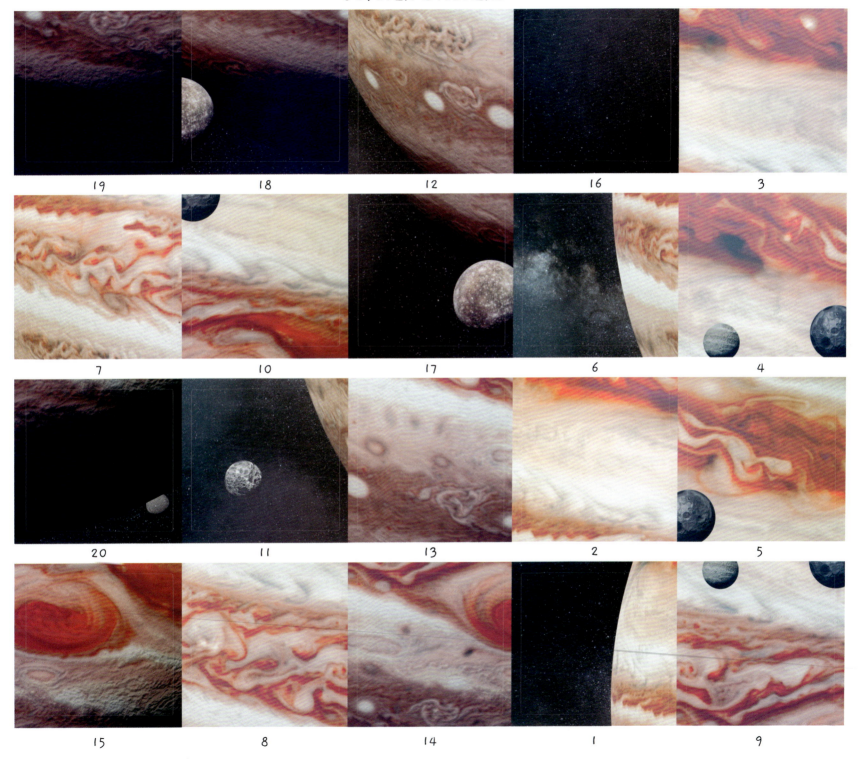

SATURN STICKERS

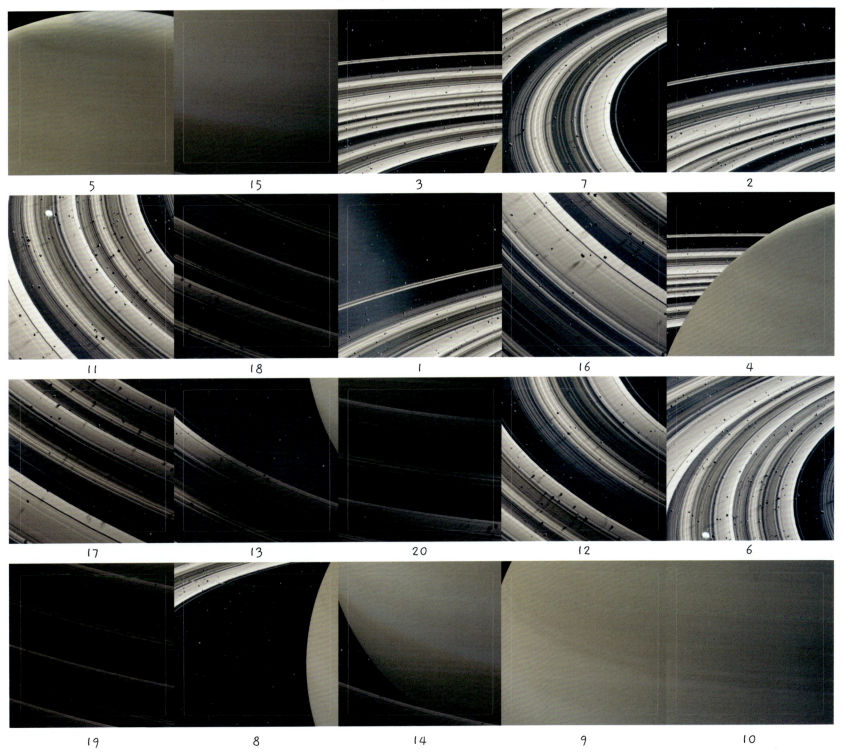

5   15   3   7   2

11   18   1   16   4

17   13   20   12   6

19   8   14   9   10

SATELLITE STICKERS

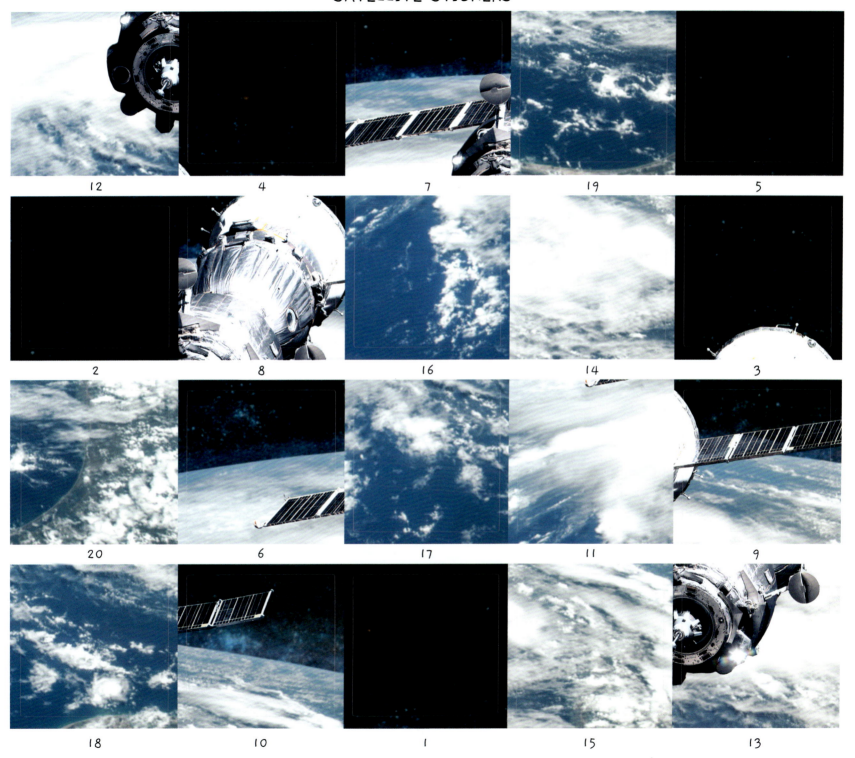

12   4   7   19   5

2   8   16   14   3

20   6   17   11   9

18   10   1   15   13

SOLAR SYSTEM STICKERS

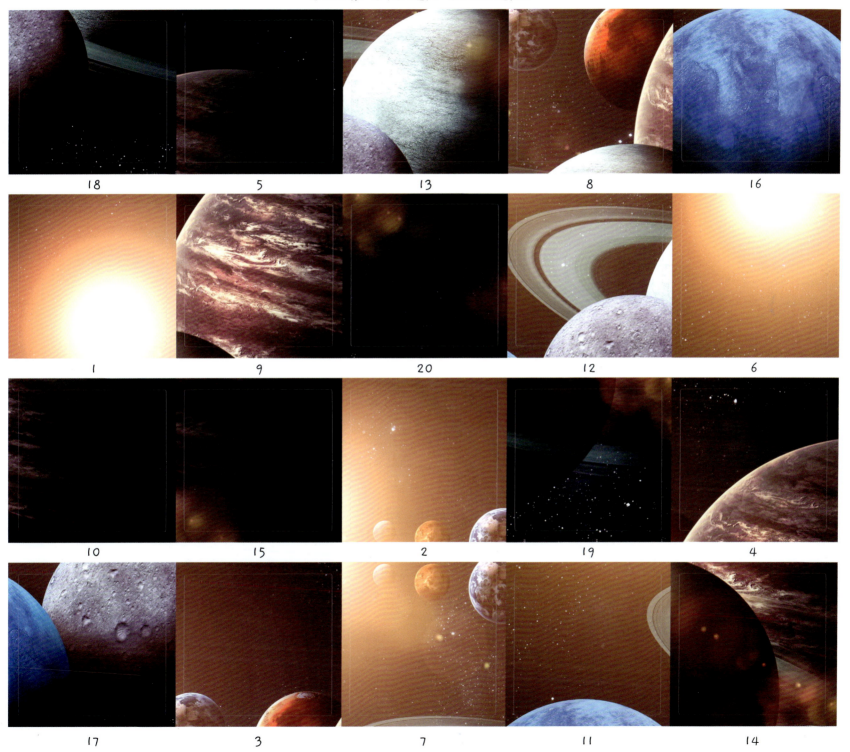